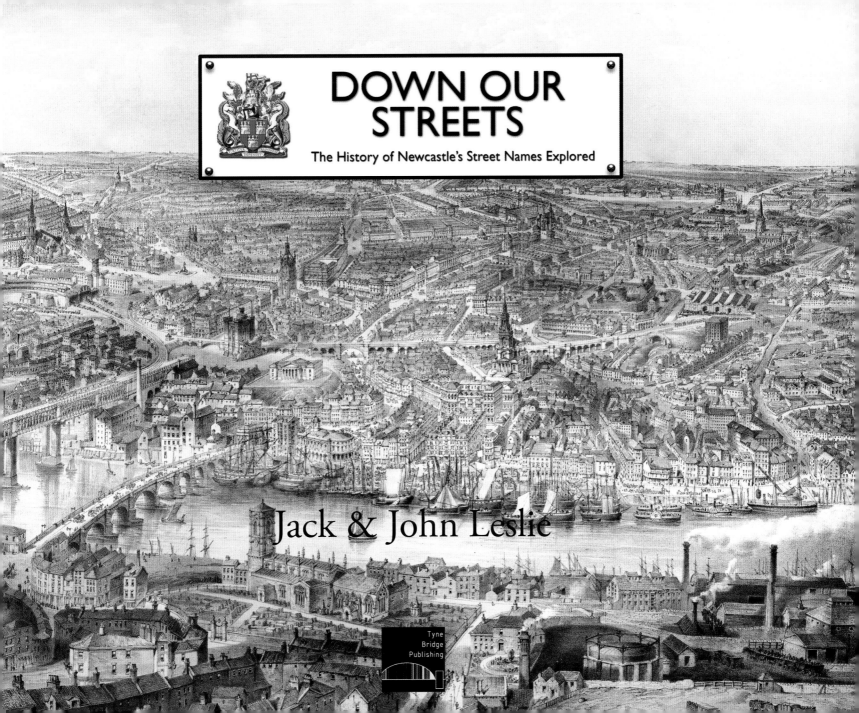

DOWN OUR STREETS

The History of Newcastle's Street Names Explored

Jack & John Leslie

Tyne Bridge Publishing

Acknowledgements

The publishers would like to thank John Grundy for generously contributing the foreword of the book. We would also like to thank Douglas Bond, Jimmy Donald and Frank Manders for their invaluable advice.

Many of the images in this new and updated edition have never been seen before. We would like to thank Fiona Kay and Neil Storey for their tireless and enthusatic work in unearthing and digitising images from the glass plate collection held at City Library, Newcastle. Other images they have unearthed will form new Tyne Bridge Publishing books.

This edition, design and additional material - David Hepworth.

Published by
Tyne Bridge Publishing 2003, 2006, 2017.
City Library
Newcastle Upon Tyne
tynebridgepublishing.org.uk

Title Page: A view of Newcastle upon Tyne in the Reign of Queen Victoria, 1862 by John Storey.

Cover images, clockwise from top left: 1) The top of Dog Leap Stairs and the Castle Garth. 2) The Tyne Bridge and Quayside 3) Grey Street from Grey's Monument. 4) A gathering in the Bigg Market.

Rear cover images, clockwise from top left: 1) A postcard of Northumberland Street. 2) A painted postcard of Grainger Street by night. 3) A view down Dog Leap Stairs to Side.

Foreword

Over the years I have spent a lot of time filming in Newcastle, trying to read the history of the place from its surviving buildings and of course I love them because there is such a wealth and such a variety among them. I now realise, however, after reading this book that I have badly underestimated a major source of interest and information – the richness locked up in the names of the streets that my favourite buildings are on. The whole history of Newcastle seems to be recorded in the very names we take for granted as we rush around town. Some streets preserve the names of the great and the good who built and influenced the town, others recall the working lives of its old inhabitants. There are streets that hold the only clue to the existence of long-lost institutions like nunneries and monasteries, still others are faint memories of the natural landscape that lies beneath the modern pavements – the ancient streams that flowed down to the Tyne and the ravines and denes they flowed through, the meadows, woods and orchards that disappeared beneath its modern expansion.

There are names of course which turn out to defy explanation (Pink Lane, oddly enough) while on the other hand there are those whose origins are painfully obvious (why are those called Long Stairs, mister?...durr!). Some of the explanations even turn out to be a bit of a disappointment (I did so want Darn Crook to have been the scene of naughty criminal doings). Some derivations ought to have been obvious but aren't. It takes a marvellous leap of the imagination to strip away the modern Sandhill with its wonderful jumble of Victorian and medieval buildings, with its underclad and rowdy revellers, with all the noise and bustle of the modern city and see in your mind's eye the original hill of sand that stood by the banks of the ancient River Tyne.

I have to admit that I have another, more selfish reason for welcoming this book. There are a few things more irritating to a show off than having to admit to ignorance. Sadly it happens to me all the time. Because they've seen me on television, people stop me and expect me to answer their unsolved questions. Why's there a mad rabbit round behind the cathedral? Did a dog ever leap down Dogleap Stairs? Do you know why that street is called Amen Corner? Who was Fenkle? I thought the Nevilles lived down south in Raby Castle, why is there a street named after them here?

I've had all of these questions and lots of others, and in the past I've failed with them all. But not anymore. This excellent guide to the street names of Newcastle will save my bacon and satisfy thousands of enquiring minds including my own …

… and then of course there are the old photos – wonderful and atmospheric shots of the old Newcastle which are worth buying in their own right.

John Grundy

Grey Street and Grey's Monument, 1928.

Jack Leslie - 1925 to 2011

Local historian and researcher Jack Leslie, whose extensive research
(mainly undertaken in Newcastle Library)
laid the bedrock for this book, passed away in 2011.

I know he felt blessed to have his work developed into a publication by Tyne Bridge
Publishing, and he was thrilled to see the initial production runs completed and
selling in book shops.

Jack would have been delighted with this, wonderfully updated, version of the book.
Jack was an intelligent, generous and hardworking man, who lived life to the full, and
was dedicated to his family.

Proud of you Dad.

John Leslie

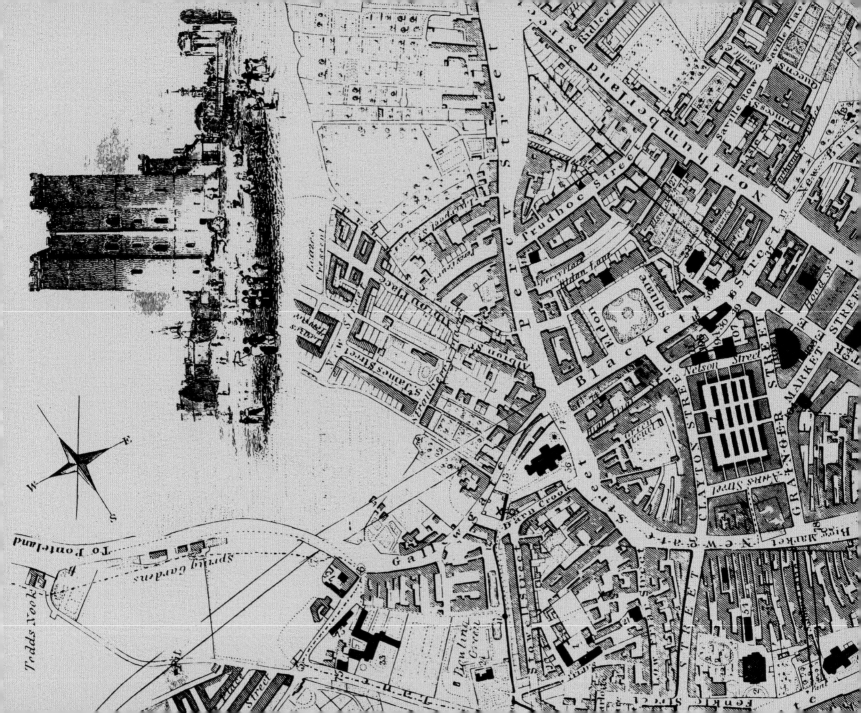

Many of the streets seen is this map of 1838 feature in this book. The City's general layout has not changed a great deal, the main thoroughfares of Pilgrim Street, Northumberland Street, Newgate Street, Blackett Street and Percy Street are still present, but many of the features seen here are gone.

As the City developed with railway lines and stations, then main roads and motorways, shopping centres and office blocks, many features disappeared. Pandon Dene was filled in - now thousands of vehicles travel along its route along the central motorway, the prison on Carliol Square is gone, as are many of the long, thin 'burgess' plots off Pilgrim Street.

SANDHILL

CAFE & COCOA ROOMS

Sandhill

Sandhill was at one time literally a hill of sand beside the river, and the street name, first mentioned in 1310 recalls this far-off time.

By the 14th century the area was a market and recreation ground. There was a bullring there until 1768, when a spectator was gored by a bull and killed and the bull ring was closed. By the 17th century the street was a fashionable place where many merchants had their dwellings. Some magnificent timber framed houses still remain, notably Bessie Surtees' House.

Sandhill's most famous story is that of Bessie Surtees, the daughter of a wealthy banker. She was in love with John Scott, son of a coal fitter, but her father disapproved of the match. In 1772, Bessie eloped with her sweetheart from a window in her father's house in Sandhill. The marriage was a long and happy one and John Scott rose to be Lord Eldon, Chancellor of England.

c1900. The Guildhall can be seen on the left of the picture. Bessie Surtees' house is in the rear - at this stage in its history the ground floor is a Café and Cocoa room.

Sandhill Views:

Clockwise from far left:

1) One of the earliest photographs taken in Newcastle, thought to be taken pre-1869. 2) People in one of the 'Entrys' off Sandhill, 1884. 3) A steam train travels across the High Level Bridge, 1954. 4) A single truck under the Tyne Bridge near the Guildhall, 1940.

The Close

The name derives from the closeness or narrowness of the street, as in the Scottish 'close'. The Close was the centre of the town in medieval times. At one time a fashionable area, the Mansion House, or Mayor's residence was situated here between 1691 and 1836. Local dignitaries including Sir John Marley, Sir William Blackett and Sir Mark Millbank also lived in The Close. Hanover, Breakneck, Tuthill and Long Stairs run up from The Close.

Skinnerburn Road

The street name comes from the Skinner Burn, one of Newcastle's many hidden waterways, which rose at the top of Bath Lane and flowed down the route of Bath Lane, across Westgate Road, down Waterloo Street and Forth Banks into the river. Coal mining probably caused the ground water table of the burn to drop. Skinnerburn Road extends westwards from the bottom of Forth banks. 'Skinner' may refer to the narrowness of the old stream.

Above: Work at the outlet of the Skinner Burn during the construction of the Queen Elizabeth Metro Bridge in 1980. Right: A train crossing the King Edward VII bridge in 1978.

Previous page: Top) An undated photograph showing sheep being driven along The Close. Bottom) Newcastle in the late 1800s, The Close is surrounded by industry and bonded warehouses. The Quayside bar is now one of the only surviving buildings of this period.

Hanover Street, Square and Stairs

Hanover Square is built on the site of a Carmelite Friary. The Carmelites were known as White Friars because of the colour of their habits. Followers of the Reverend Benjamin Bennett purchased the site in about 1720 to erect a Unitarian Chapel and a square of houses. The name honours the royal family, the House of Hanover. George 1, the first Hanover king came to the throne in 1714.

Hanover Street leads up from the western end of the Close past the site of the bonded warehouses and the top of Hanover Stairs. Nearer the top of the street is Breakneck Stairs and opposite the top of these stood the White Friars Tower, which was in the section of the Town Wall leading to Forth Street. The tower and a section of the Town Wall were demolished when Hanover Street was built.

Above: Hanover Square in the 1880s. Right: Hanover Street still cobbled in 1989, many of the bonded warehouses are now demolished.

Forth Street and Forth Banks

The name 'Forth 'is derived from 'Frith', meaning a pasture or shaded place. Forth Banks and Forth Street are associated with an area known as the Forth from medieval times, just outside the west Town Wall. The Forth was being used for recreational activities, including archery, in the mid-16th century. In the mid-17th century an order was taken out to lease the Forth and paddock adjoining it as a bowling green for twenty-one years at a rent not exceeding £21 per annum. By the 18th century it included formal walks, Forth Walks.

Thomas Bewick the artist and engraver, lived near Forth Walks from 1781 to 1811. Previously a pleasant place to live, the Forth rapidly became built up and a centre of industry during the 19th century. The Central Station and Neville Street now cover it.

Forth Banks, 1900.

South Street

This street appears to have been named simply because it runs south from Forth Street.

South Street was the site of Robert Stephenson & Co.'s engineering works, which produced the world-famous *Rocket*. Robert and his father, George, were partners in the firm, which, when it was established in 1823, was the only purpose-built locomotive factory in the world.

Next to Stephenson's works was the engineering company of Robert and William Hawthorn, who began making locomotives in 1832. In the great railway boom of the 1830s and 1840s, these two firms were major suppliers, and in 1937 the locomotive department of Hawthorn Leslie amalgamated with Stephenson's to become Robert Stephenson & Hawthorns Ltd.

South Street - Stephenson's engineering works.

Orchard Street

An orchard, which was tended by the Carmelite religious order, once occupied this area. In fact there were orchards on both sides of the west Tower Wall. A section of the wall still stands here today. A nearby demolished tower, Spital Tower, was named after the Hospital of the Blessed Virgin Mary, which was surrounded by the orchards. Building in Orchard Street began in 1812.

Clavering Place

This street was renamed in 1784 after Sir Thomas Clavering Bart, of Axwell. Property in the street was bought for him after his marriage to the daughter of Joshua Douglas, the Town Clerk. In 1754 Sir Thomas was a Member of Parliament for Shaftesbury. He served as MP for County Durham from 1768.

(The) Side

The Side, or just plain Side, as it is traditionally called, is not only one of the shortest street names but one of the most ancient thoroughfares in Newcastle, and until Dean Street was constructed in the 1780s, it was the main route from the riverside to the higher part of town and beyond.

According to the historian John Brand, the street got its name because it is a route down the side of a hill and because of its proximity to the Castle. Although it was one of the town's principal streets, it was not particularly salubrious. In 1807, a correspondent to the Gentleman's Magazine wrote "The Street called 'The Side' would be a disgrace to any Corporation in England". However, one of Newcastle's most famous sons, Admiral Collingwood was born on the site of Milburn House (built 1902-5) on 26 September, 1748. The street is mentioned in Bourne's History of Newcastle, where it was stated that "the thoroughfare known as the Side bore three separate names". The three parts of the street were known as, Side, Cordwainers Raw and Flesher Raw.

Side c1900. The buildings in the centre of the image were replaced by Milburn House in 1902.

SIDE

Side Images:

Top left: Opened in 1905, Milburn House at the junction of Side and Dean Street now blocks the view of the cathedral. Above: Side in 1880 showing Lockhart's Cocoa Rooms. Left: The top of Side near Amen Corner. Next page: Side seen in 1893.

St Nicholas Street

This street, constructed c.1851 to lead to the High Level Bridge, takes its name from St Nicholas Church, founded by Osamund, Bishop of Salisbury in 1091. In 1216 the church was burned down and it was re-built in 1353. It became a cathedral in 1882.

In 1828 the Newcastle Post Office was moved from Mosley Street to the west side of St Nicholas' churchyard. The 1828 façade has been retained during its refurbishment as flats in 2001.

On the eastern side of St Nicholas Street stands the Black Gate. This was the principal entrance to the Castle and was built between 1247 and 1250. It is called after Patrick Black, a London Merchant who leased the gatehouse in the 17th century and lived there with his wife Barbara.

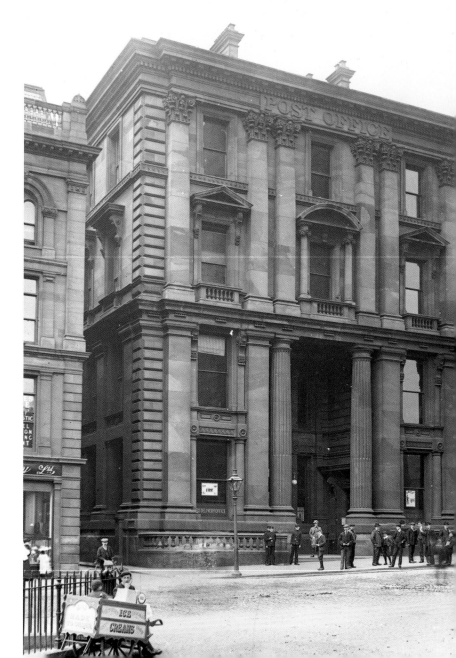

The General Post Office on St Nicholas Street complete with ice cream seller in the foreground.

Amen Corner

The corner of the south side of St Nicholas Churchyard with Side, Amen Corner has a religious association. Clergy used to hold a procession around the outside of the cathedral, praying as they went. Amen Corner is where they came to the end of the prayer.

The workshops of Ralph Beilby, the enamel painter, jeweller and engraver were located here. Thomas Bewick was apprenticed to Beilby from 1767 to 1774, returning to go into partnership with his old master in 1777. In 1795 he moved to a new workshop in the south-east corner of St Nicholas Churchyard, and in 1797 the partnership with Beilby was formally dissolved. Newcastle's first circulating library was here too, established by Joseph Barber in 1746 from his house on the corner.

On the back wall of one of the Edwardian Cathedral Buildings, which front on to Dean Street looking west over the churchyard, is an improbable stone rabbit, with a wild expression and worryingly long teeth! Nobody seems to know why it is there.

Amen Corner - the small lane running along the south side of the churchyard.

Newcastle's Stairs

The Castle stairs lead directly from The Close to Castle Garth. On the south side of the Castle Garth is the Moot Hall, which stands almost on the site of the medieval Great Hall of the King, or Moot Hall, where the business of local government was carried out. An anomaly meant the Castle Garth area became an island of Northumberland in the middle of Newcastle for many years, and consequently was the haunt of criminals on the run from the Newcastle authorities. The Northumberland Assizes were held in the Moot Hall. The foundation stone of the present building was laid on 22nd July 1810 (with permission to erect gallows for Northumberland there) and it was completed in 1812 at a cost of £60,000. When walking down Castle Stairs you can see small green plots to the left and right. These are the remains of the gardens of the Merchants' houses on the Quayside. Castle Stairs was famous for its shoemakers and clog makers.

The Long Stairs are named because they were the longest set of stairs leading up from the Quayside, Long Stairs lead up from The Close to Queen's Lane and the entrance to the High Level Bridge. The quaintly named Sheep Head Alley, probably so-called because of the livestock trade on the Quayside, forms part of the path that joins Long Stairs to Castle Stairs.

Over the years there have been many different spellings of Tuthill Stairs. These include Tooterhill, Tudhill and Touthill. It is said that the name comes from 'touting' or 'winding' of a horn by a lookout when enemies were approaching the town. In 1859 there were houses, a chapel and businesses including a slater and grocers on these stairs.

Breakneck Stairs form part of the western Town Wall, which tumbles down the sharply inclined slope from the demolished White Friar Tower to the Close. They presumably got their name because they were extremely steep and therefore hazardous. Close Gate was situated where Breakneck Stairs meets the road. A plaque on the north wall of the Close marks its location. Breakneck Stairs can be seen today but they are not accessible to the public.

People have always lived on the steep slopes of the Tyne but living space has always been in short supply so close to the river. Castle Stairs, Long Stairs, and Hanover Stairs can be seen on Speed's map of 1610. Largely constructed from tough Scottish granite, the stairs contained dwellings, tradesmen, shops, wells and gardens. They have been rebuilt, built over and altered over the years but many clues to their history remain. On Castle Stairs, a popular route to the upper town for pedestrians before the High Level Bridge was built, there is a restored medieval well on the first landing.

Before the 19th century, Dog Leap Stairs were so narrow that a dog could leap across them. However, 'dog loup', a narrow slip of land between houses, indicates the shape of a dog's hind leg which, since the stairs have a twist, could equally well be the derivation. They were widened in 1822. The stairs led from the east side of the crowded dwellings of the Castle Garth, now an open area beside the Black Gate, to join Dean Street at the foot of Side.

Next page, clockwise from top left. 1) Castle Stairs through the southern postern, featuring clogmakers, 1930. 2) The foot of Tuthill Stairs. 3) Tuthill Stairs, 1960.

JOHN

DOG LEAP STAIRS

SIDE

From Neville Street to Blackett Street

This part of the city is bounded to the west by Blenheim Street and to the east by Grainger Street. Development here started in the 18th century and the area contains important buildings such as Newcastle Central Station, the Grainger Market, St Mary's Roman Catholic Cathedral and the Old Assembly Rooms. Architect Thomas Oliver noted that "the new Roman Catholic Chapel of St Mary's had the foundation stone laid on 4th March 1843" and that the tower was to be erected on the west side.

Neville Street

Built in 1835 to provide easier communication between Collingwood Street and the Cattle Market on Scotswood Road, Neville Street included two towers of the Town Wall. Nearby was the Denton Tower or Neville Tower from which the street takes its name. The tower was named after the Neville family, Earls of Westmorland who had a seat at Raby Castle, County Durham. The Nevilles had a town house, Westmorland Place, on the site of the present Literary and Philosophical Society.

Neville Street was widened in 1847-8 to make way for John Dobson's Central Station and the opening of the Newcastle and Berwick Railway. Queen Victoria officially opened the station in 1850. Before that, the 'Newcastle Terminus' had been a temporary station west of its present site.

Top) The locomotive Puffing Billy *near Stephenson's Monument.*
Right) Neville Street decorated for the King's visit in 1906.

Neville Street showing the Central Station and St Mary's Cathedral. Oyster bars occupy the buildings near the bottom of Pink Lane.

25

Neville Street, 1900.

Pink Lane

Near to the present junction of Pink Lane and Clayton Street West stood Pink Tower, one of the seventeen round towers on the wall. Pink Lane, which followed the line of the wall was named after the tower. Exactly why the tower had that name is unknown. The wall, constructed from 1265, was 7-10 feet thick and between 20 and 30 feet high. Pink Lane was part of the 'pomerium', a narrow land running inside the wall to give defenders access to it, and on which it was illegal to build. Pink Tower was removed in 1852 to make way for John Knox Chapel. The image on the right shows Pink Lane in 1965.

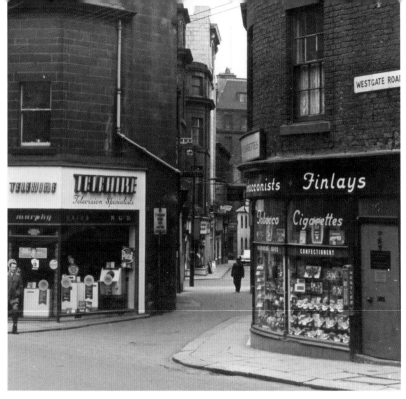

Bewick Street

Thomas Bewick, for whom this street is named, was born at Cherryburn, near Prudhoe in 1753 and after serving his apprenticeship with Ralph Beilby, the celebrated metal and glass engraver of Amen Corner, he became a partner in the firm.

Bewick spent most of his working life engraving on metal but he is best remembered for his wood engravings, many of which, such as the Chillingham Bull, are still justly famous today. A bronze commemorative plaque of the Chillingham Bull is now installed on Bewick Street to commemorate the site of the house on the Forth where Bewick lived as an established engraver between 1781 and 1811. He would walk to work along Forth Lane and down Westgate Road. You can see the town boundary stone in Forth Lane. The image shows Bewick Street and St Mary's Cathedral.

Blenheim Street

Many towns honour national heroes and events by naming streets after them – Blenheim Street is named after the Duke of Marlborough's great victory over the French in 1704.

The image shows Blenheim Street in the 1950s, this area is now St James's Boulevard.

Waterloo Street

Waterloo Street runs south from the junction of Bath Lane and Westgate Road. The Waterloo Inn stood on this corner from the 18th century until it was demolished in 2001 to allow for redevelopment of the area. The inn and the street are named after the famous battle of 1815.

This image shows the Cooperative Wholesale Society premises on Waterloo Street and Thornton Street.

Westgate Road

Westgate Road was first of all just Westgate, from the Norse 'geat' or road towards the west. It then became Westgate Street, and later Road. The West Gate, one of the strongly fortified gates in the Town Wall, stood at the present junction of Pink Lane and Westgate Road. There was a thoroughfare to the west at least one hundred years before the Town Wall was built.

Beyond the gate lay Northumberland and the gallows that was used for the execution of prisoners found guilty of murder at the Northumberland Assizes. A law passed in 1750 meant that such prisoners had to be hanged soon after their trial so there was not time to take them to Morpeth Gaol. On the 10th August 1792 a triple execution took place when William Winter, Janet Clark and Eleanor Clark were hanged for murdering an old woman, Margaret Crosier, near Elsdon in Northumberland. Winter's body was subsequently hung in chains on Harwood Moor as an example to others.

Below) The bottom of Westgate Road with the Stephenson Monument, St Nicholas Cathedral and the Mining Institute on the right.
Right) The top image shows Westgate Road in 1886, the lower image shows the same pillar in 2017.

Bath Lane

In 1781 public medical baths were built in Newcastle. These baths, which were a private venture, contained a large swimming bath as well as traditional Buxton vapour baths. The baths stood near Westgate Road, giving Bath Lane its name. The image shows bath lane in 1897.

Cross Street

Charles Hutton's map of 1769 shows this street as Ratten Row (Rotten Row). It is not certain why it became Cross Street, but one possibility is that it simply 'crossed' between Westgate Road and Low Friar Street. The image shows the junction of Cross Street, Westgate Road and Pink Lane.

Fenkle Street

Previously called Fennel or Fenchale Street, this term means corner or the corner of a street, therefore many 'fenkle streets' can be found in Newcastle. Fenkle also means a stream; an open gutter ran down Fenkle Street for many years. Alternatively, the street may be named after Nicholas Fenkell, a 16th century merchant. The Assembly Rooms were opened on the junction of Westgate Road and Fenkle Street in 1776. They were a meeting place for Newcastle's fashionable society and were the venue for balls, concerts and other entertainments. The Tyne Theatre and Opera House was opened on Westgate Road in 1867.

The image shows Fenkle Street in 1897.

Clayton Street

The street was completed in 1841 as the final part of the scheme for town improvement started by Richard Grainger. It was named after John Clayton (1792-1890), who was Town Clerk for many years and a leading supporter of the new developments. It was largely due to his foresight and interest that the grandiose scheme proposed by Richard Grainger was carried out.

The image on the right has been augmented with paint at some time to bring out the highlights of the firemen.

Low Friar Street

This street was formerly called Shod-Friar Chare, so named because of its proximity to the Black (or Shod) Friars' (Dominicans) monastery. The name Shod-Friar is associated with the religious order of monks who wore shoes, rather than going barefoot. From the 13th century it was called Low Friar Street. It's hard to imagine that the 1886 image on the right shows the area near the heart of China Town and The Gate complex.

Dispensary Lane

Before there was any organised medical service in Newcastle, poor people had to rely upon the free medical help that was available at the town's dispensary. The Newcastle Dispensary was started in 1777 in Side and subsequently moved to Pilgrim Street. By 1790 it had moved to a site off Low Friar Street, giving Dispensary Lane its name. In 1893 the dispensary moved to Nelson Street and finally to New Bridge Street in 1928, where it remained until its closure in 1976. The image on the left is from 1935.

Stowell Street

John Scott, later Lord Eldon, and husband of Bessie Surtees, was the most famous member of the Scott family, but his elder brother William, who was born in Heworth, became an eminent judge whose judgements in maritime law are still used as precedents. He was created Baron Stowell and Stowell Street, built by Young in 1820 as a street of town houses, was named in his honour. William Scott and John Scott each had a twin sister. William's sister Barbara lived until she was 77, but John's sister Elizabeth died shortly after their birth in Love Lane on Newcastle Quayside.

The top image shows the Green Fruit Department of the Cooperative Wholesale Society, the bottom picture shows the same building in the heart of modern China Town.

Gallowgate

The name is a corruption of 'Gallows Gate', not the name of a gate in the Town Wall, but the road or 'geat' used to take convicted criminals to the Newcastle gallows for execution. Gallows stood on Newcastle Town Moor from 1480. One of the last people to be hanged on the Town Moor was Mark Sherwood in 1844, for the murder of his wife in Blandford Street.

The street is no longer a route to the gallows but it is one of the main routes to St James's Park, the home of Newcastle United Football Club.

Newgate Street

The New Gate at the junction of Newgate Street and Gallowgate was the principal gate of the six in the Town Wall and probably the strongest as it faced the north and Scotland. From 1400 onwards it housed the town gaol. The demolition of the New Gate began in 1823, and in 1824 the Town Wall running from this area to the east was removed to enable the building of Blackett Street and Eldon Square. St Andrew's Church is the city's oldest church, first appearing in the records in 1218.

Darn Crook
(St Andrew's Street)

Now called St Andrew's Street because of its closeness to St Andrew's Church, its former name of Darn Crook is still used by many locals. The origins of the strange name are obscure but probably refer to the dark and crooked or twisted lane. Until 1810 the street was a cul-de-sac blocked at the north by the Town Wall. It was here in 1644, during the Civil War, that the Scots under General Baillie breached the wall and invaded the town.

Previous Page: Top) Gallowgate in 1915, the scene of a fatal steam wagon accident. Bottom) Newgate Street in 1911 decorated for the coronation of King George V and Queen Mary. H. Samuel (Jewellers) is in the foreground with Grainger Street on the right. The 'Albion' public house (now the Rose and Crown) is next to the Empire Palace theatre. Right: Darn Crook or St Andrew's Street in 1950. A section of the Town Wall can be seen of the left.

Above) St Andrew's Church, 1890. Next Page) The Coop on Newgate Street in 1946.

39

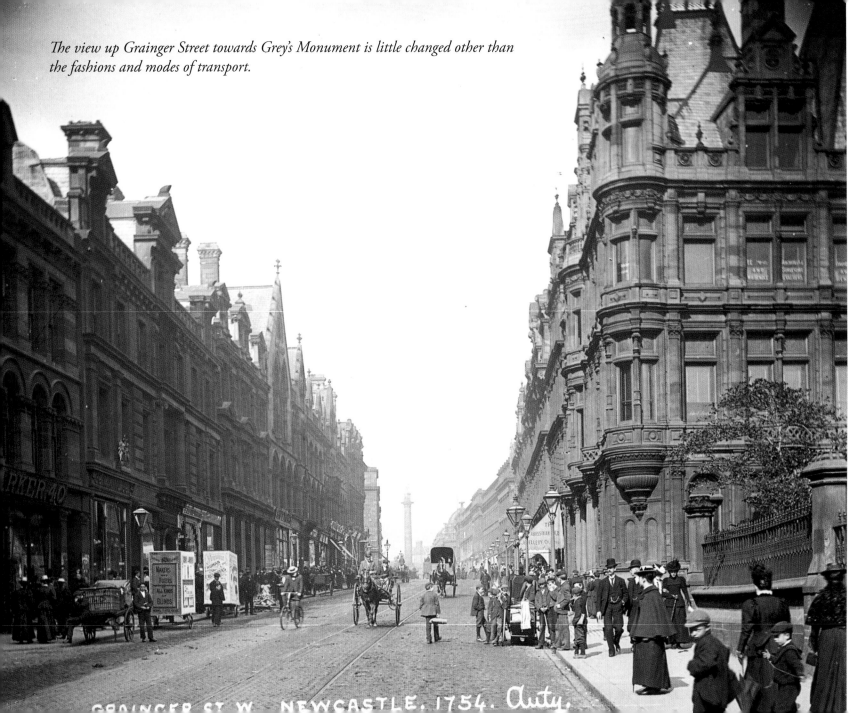

The view up Grainger Street towards Grey's Monument is little changed other than the fashions and modes of transport.

GRAINGER ST W. NEWCASTLE. 1754. Auty.

Grainger Street

This street was named after Richard Grainger (1797-1861), entrepreneur, builder and planner of much of the city centre as we see it today. It was built in the 1830s. Grainger Street West, which runs from Bigg Market to Neville Street, was not built until 1868. Before that it was a narrow alley leading past St John's Church. The son of a porter, Grainger started a house building business with his brother. Later, with the support of John Clayton the Town Clerk and the architect John Dobson, he undertook ambitious building projects in Newcastle. Grainger was born in High Friar Lane, which disappeared with the construction of Eldon Square Shopping Centre. It ran parallel to Blackett Street.

Nelson Street

This is another of the streets built by Richard Grainger. Its name commemorates Lord Nelson, hero of Trafalgar, just as Collingwood Street commemorates his second in command. The façade of a 19th century music hall has been retained in Nelson Street. Richard Grainger laid the foundation stone in 1829. In this music hall, in the winter of 1861, Charles Dickens gave readings from his novels, *David Copperfield, Nicholas Nickleby,* and *Little Dombey* (adapted from the early chapters of *Dombey and Son*). Seats were very expensive, at between one and four shillings, although poorer people were allowed in the standing gallery for a penny. Not surprising, then, that Dickens wrote to a friend: "At Newcastle against heavy expenses, I made more than a hundred guineas profit". However, money was not the only reason Dickens enjoyed his visit to Newcastle. He wrote: "A finer audience there is not in England, and I suppose them to be a specially earnest people; for while they can laugh until they shake the roof, they have a very unusual sympathy with what is pathetic or passionate".

During a reading of *David Copperfield*, Dickens showed remarkable composure when a 'gas batten' came crashing down from above him and the audience began to surge I panic. As a lady ran towards the stage Charles Dickens calmly said "There's nothing the matter, I assure you; don't be alarmed, pray sit down", at which point she returned to her seat to thunderous applause from the audience.

Grainger Street, 1890.

Nun Street

Near the present Nun Street, and giving its name to the street, stood a Benedictine Nunnery, The Priory of Saint Bartholomew, the first convent established in Newcastle. The Priory owned land throughout the area, their immediate grounds being the Nuns Field on which Richard Grainger built several of his new streets and the Grainger Market. Where Nun Street meets Nuns Lane there was an entrance to the convent.

Blackett Street

Before the redevelopment of 1824, this street was a muddy lane running westwards from Pilgrim Street, lined with gardens and middens. As part of Richard Grainger's improvements, it became a major thoroughfare with elegant new houses. The new street was named after John Erasmus Blackett (1728 – 1814) who was Mayor of Newcastle on four occasions during the 18th century. This view (right) from 1955 is very different from what we see today, the entrance the the food mall of Eldon Square occupies the site of the YMCA, you can see Emerson Chambers on the right where Waterstone's is sells books in 2017.

Previous page) A view of the junction of Northumberland Street and Blackett Street from 1911.
Above) An 1895 view east along Blackett Street.

Grainger Market

This is a covered market, a shopping mall of its time, lying between Nun Street and Nelson Street, built by Richard Grainger. On 22nd October 1835, some 200 townsfolk attended a high banquet in the market to celebrate its opening.

The market covered an area of 13,906 square yards with dimensions of 338 feet 3 inches by 241 feet 7 inches. The cost of this market to the Corporation was £36,290.

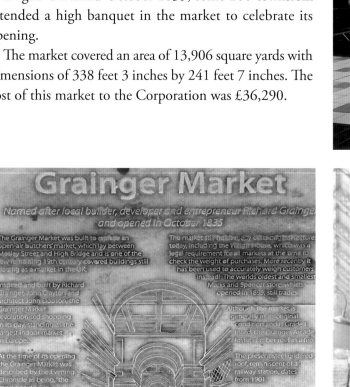

North of Blackett Street

This chapter covers an area that in modern times has seen many changes. The most notable development is the Eldon Square shopping centre, which involved the reconstruction of large parts of central Newcastle. In addition the Haymarket area has been developed with a modern bus terminus at its centre. The hospital of Mary Magdelene stood in this area until 1828 when St Thomas Church replaced it.

Elspeth Rutter

Leazes Terrace, Leazes Lane, Leazes Park Road

Leazes is an Old English name meaning to glean or gather and in Newcastle the Leazes refers to green pastures reserved for hay cropping. Castle Leazes (a gift from King John to the Mayor and burgesses of Newcastle), the Town Moor and Nuns Moor are all areas of common pasture outside the old town wall. The burgesses allowed part of this land to be used for building from the 18th century and in 1895 St James's Park Football Ground was built on the Leazes for the newly formed Newcastle United Football Club. Leazes Park opened in 1873, was Newcastle's first public park.

The fine restored houses in Leazes Crescent and Terrace were designed by Thomas Oliver in the early 1830s. Before 1895 Leazes Park Road was known as Albion Road.

Top) Leazes Lane in the 1970s. Right) Ranch boutique at the bottom of Leazes Lane.

Percy Street

Originally known as Sidgate (the road to the Side), this ancient street had been renamed Percy Street by the 18th century. The name, considered to be more refined than Sidgate, derives from the Percy family, whose seat has been Alnwick Castle since 1309.

This section of Percy Street near the junction with Leazes Park Road, is unrecognisable from the modern street scene.

St Thomas's Street and Crescent

St Thomas's Street and Crescent, built in the 1840s, are named after St Thomas's Chapel, which stood at the Newcastle end of the Tyne Bridge. In 1660 the chapel united with the leper hospital of Mary Magdelene, which was situated at Barras Bridge where St Thomas's church stands now. The chapel was demolished in 1830. St Thomas's Church, which replaced both the hospital and the chapel, was designed by John Dobson and built between 1828 and 1830. Behind 3 St Thomas's Crescent is a studio used by the artist William Bell Scott. Dante Gabriel Rossetti visited him there in 1853.

From 1683 to 1790, an area of ground bordered by St Thomas's Street , Percy Street and the Hotspur Breweries, was used as a burial site. The site was 200 feet by 40 feet and is shown on Charles Hutton's map of Newcastle dated 1772.

Showing St Thomas's Crescent with St James's Park, Leazes Terrace and Todd's Nook flats in background.

Haymarket

The area takes its name from a weekly market established in 1824 for the sale of hay and straw on the east side of Percy Street. It was closed as a haymarket in the 1930s. The ground was used for many purposes, including open air meetings, menageries and hirings for local farms.

Barras Bridge

The Pandon Burn, one of several streams whose deep ravines originally divided Newcastle, rose north of Newcastle and flowed through the east side of the town into the Tyne. A bridge was built to carry the main route north over this burn. The bridge itself was raised, rebuilt and widened in 1819 and although the valley was filled in later in the century, the stone Barras Bridge still survives underground as part of Newcastle's system of sewers. The name Barras probably derives from 'barrows' or burial mounds belonging to the leper hospital of Saint Mary Magdalene.

Clockwise from top. 1) A colourful 1950's postcard showing St Thomas's Church and the Northumbrian Regiments Boer War Memorial. 2) A drawing showing Barras Bridge. 3) A coloured postcard showing Barras Bridge near 'The Response' War memorial.

St Mary's Place

It was the custom in the middle ages to locate leper hospitals well outside the Town Walls. These hospitals were usually charitable foundations. One was the Hospital of St Mary Magdalene, which stood on the site of the present St Thomas's Church. St Mary's Place took its name from this foundation and the Trustees of the St Mary Magdalene Charity still own the land (see the plaque in the grounds of St Thomas's Church).

The photograph shows the junction of St Mary's Place and Northumberland Street, the building on the corner was a Singer sewing machine shop, today it is occupied by TSB Bank. Many buildings in the background made way for Newcastle Civic Centre and buildings for the University of Northumbria.

Ridley Place

Built by Grey and Mackford in the early 19th century, this street is named after the Ridley family of Blagdon hall and Newcastle. Many members of this ancient family have served as Members of Parliament, Mayors and Councillors.

Ellison Place

Ellison Place was named after the Ellison family. Cuthbert Ellison was Sheriff of Newcastle in 1544 and Mayor in 1549 and 1554. In 1866 No.1 Ellison Place was purchased by the Corporation to be used as lodgings for visiting judges. In 1886 it became Newcastle's second Mansion House. This street is a continuation of Saville Place.

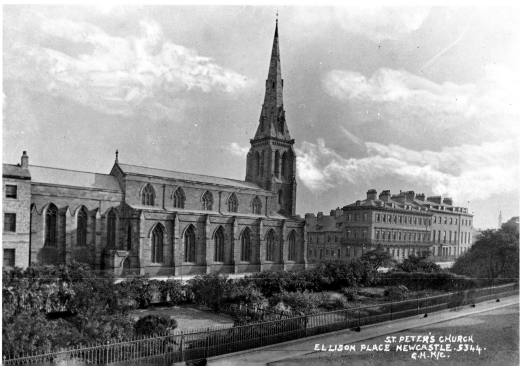

John Dobson Street

John Dobson was born in 1787 sat North Shields and, after serving his apprenticeship with David Stephenson (the architect of Dean Street, Mosley Street and All Saints' Church), he established himself in Newcastle as a professional architect in about 1810. Dobson was one of several local architects working at the beginning of the 19th century who gave Newcastle many streets of fine stone-faced buildings in a style that has been termed Tyneside Classical.

Dobson worked with Richard Grainger, planning many of his new streets, the best of which is probably Grey Street. Dobson's buildings are to be found throughout the North East and his genius may be seen in Newcastle in such buildings as St Thomas's Church, Old Eldon Square, The Lying in Hospital (now a commercial building in New Bridge Street) and the Central Railway Station. The street bearing his name was built in the 1960s to relieve the pressure of traffic on Northumberland Street, the image shows John Dobson street soon after opening.

Saville Row and Saville Place

These were once streets of fashionable houses, some of the first to be built outside the old Town Walls, in the latter part of the 18th century. The streets, built around 1770 were named after Sir George Saville who owned property here.

The photo of a vintage car rally on John Dobson Street was taken in 1970, the tower of the Laing Art Gallery can be seen in the background.

Eldon Square

Eldon Square is a vast indoor shopping and recreation complex, but it is named for Old Eldon Square, a magnificent Georgian Square of which only one side now survives, off Blackett Street. It was once the elegant showpiece of the improvements carried out in Newcastle by Grainger and Dobson in 1825-31. It was named after John Scott, Lord Eldon and was mostly demolished in the 1960s to make way for the new shopping centre named after it.

Although Eldon Square is a modern shopping complex, the names of the malls all link modern Newcastle with its historic past.

High Friars

High Friars Street ran almost parallel with Blackett Street, from just inside the Newgate to the house of the Franciscans or Grey Friars, which stood near the present site of Lloyds Bank on Grey Street. This street was demolished when the Eldon Square shopping centre was built, but the link with the Franciscans, who first came to Newcastle in the 13th century, has been remembered in the name of the street.

Hotspur Way, Douglas Way, Chevy Chase

These three names commemorate the bloody Battle of Otterburn, which was fought between Scots raiders and supporters of the Earl of Northumberland in August 1388. The Scots were led by James, Earl of Douglas. The Earl of Northumberland's forces were led by his son Henry, known as Harry Hotspur because of his hot-headedness in battle. The events of the battle, which ended in a resounding defeat for the English, were recorded in a poem called *The Battle of Chevy Chase*. Harry Hotspur was immortalised in the works of William Shakespeare.

Prudhoe Chare

In 1822 Prudhoe Street was built linking Percy Street and Northumberland Street as the town extended northwards. Previously there had been a bowling green on this site. The street was named after a 19th century member of the Percy family, Algernon, 4th Duke of Northumberland, who entered the House of Lords in 1816 as Lord Prudhoe. He died at Alnwick Castle at the age of seventy-three. Prudhoe Chare is built near the route of the original Prudhoe Street.

Whitecross Way

Traditionally, many of Newcastle's early markets were held at the medieval market cross, or White Cross near the Newgate. The Cross existed as early as 1400 but was pulled down in 1773. David Stephenson built a new Market Cross in 1783 and this was moved to the new Flesh Market in 1807. The site of the original cross used to be marked by a white cross painted on the mini roundabout at the junction of Newgate Street and Low Friar Street before The Gate complex was built.

Clockwise from top left. 1) A view from the now demolished YMCA of 'old' Eldon Square. 2) A photograph marking the area of the first phase to be demolished to make way for Eldon Square shopping centre. 3) The entrance to Eldon Square from Northumberland Street in the 1990s. 4) Denton's Restaurant in High Friars in Eldon Square, 1980s.

Brunswick Place

At the west end of Brunswick Place is the Brunswick Methodist Chapel, which was opened in 1821. It is from this chapel that the street takes its name. Brunswick was a popular name given to Methodist Chapels during the 18th century and there are Brunswick churches in many English cities including Liverpool, Leeds and Hull. The name commemorates the marriage of the Prince Regent to Princess Caroline of Brunswick in 1795. The Methodists were grateful to the prince for his support in legalising the position of Methodism in 1812.

Northumberland Street

A continuation of Pilgrim Street, this is one of the city's major streets, named in honour of the Duke of Northumberland. In the 18th century it was a street of well-to-do three storey brick houses leading north from the Pilgrim Street Gate, but as the commercial centre of the town grew away from the river more shops and business premises were established there. It is now one of Newcastle's main shopping streets. It became a major artery carrying through traffic north from Pilgrim Street, particularly following the opening of the Tyne Bridge in 1928, and many will remember traffic jams, traffic congestion, and narrow pavements during the 1960s. It is now pedestrianised.

The image on the right shows 'Cook's Corner' at around of the turn of the century - the below image shows that view in 2017.

In the 1950s, the A1 ran up and down Northumberland Street.

East of Grainger Street

New Bridge Street

This street, which follows the line of the town wall, ran to the New Bridge, built in 1812 to span the Pandon Burn, one of the streams that dissected the town. The bridge was demolished in the 1880s when the burn was filled in.

The image on the right shows the Pearl Buildings on the junction with Northumberland Street, the old Library and Laing Art Gallery. Manors train sheds and Hoults Removals building can be seen in the background.

Pilgrim Street

Pilgrim Street is one of the oldest streets in Newcastle. It was named because pilgrims travelling to the shrine of 'Our Lady of Jesmond' walked up this street and through Pilgrim Gate. There were many inns here to cater for the pilgrims – one was actually called The Pilgrims. The Pilgrim Gate was removed in 1802 because the arch obstructed the passage of wagons. In a rather baffling attempt to improve public health, it was also claimed that the gate "interrupted the free circulation of air in the town"!

St Andrew's Roman Catholic Chapel was opened in Pilgrim Street in 1798. The founder and first priest of this chapel was the Reverend James Worswick (see Worswick Street).

Hood Street

One of the new streets built by Richard Grainger in the 1830s, Hood Street was named after John Lionel Hood (1799 – 1848), who was the last Mayor before the municipal Corporations Act in 1835 led to changes in the structure of local government. Hood, who was mayor in 1825 and 1835, was a member of the Company of Hostmen, one of the most important of the Newcastle Trade Guilds, which controlled the monopoly of the coal trade and whose members dominated local politics before 1835.

The buildings shown at the end of Hood Street in this 1912 image were replaced with Commercial Union House.

Market Street

The scheme for the improvement of Newcastle put forward by Richard Grainger involved the demolition of the New Flesh Market, which had been opened as recently as 1808 on the upper part of the levelled dene of the Lort Burn. The small lane running off Pilgrim Street called Market Lane originally ran to this Flesh Market. In order to compensate for the loss of the newly built market, Grainger agreed to build a new covered market for the sale of meat and vegetables. It now bears his name – Grainger Market. He also built a new street, which is just north of the Grainger Market, called Market Street.

Carliol Square

Carliol Square was named after the wealthy medieval family whose members were prominent citizens and held the offices of Bailiff and Mayor in the 13th and 14th centuries. The Carels or Carliols are said to have founded the Franciscan Friary, which stood near the site of the present Lloyds TSB Bank in Grey Street. The family also gave its name to one of the towers on the Town Wall and to the Carliol Croft, an orchard that ran inside the wall on the site now occupied by Carliol House. Carliol Tower was demolished to make way for the original Newcastle Central Library, which was opened there in 1880. The present City Library in Princess Square preserves some fragments of the Carliol Tower.

In the 1820s, John Dobson built a new prison for Newcastle in Carliol Square. It replaced Newgate, and it was planned with care to reflect the most up-to-date ideas on the treatment of offenders. Unfortunately, by the time it opened its doors, theories had changed again, and Dobson's prison came in for much criticism. The prison was demolished in the 1920s and the Telephone Exchange was built on the site.

The area shown in this image on the right was totally subsumed by the Swan House Roundabout and central motorway development, but the railings in the picture are still in place.

High Bridge

Until the valley of the Lort Burn, which ran from Castle Leazes to the Tyne, was filled in, two bridges, including the Upper Dean Bridge, spanned it. High Bridge marks the site of the Upper Dean Bridge that connected Pilgrim Street with the Bigg Market.

Worswick Street

This street is named after the Reverend James Worswick, who founded the first post-Reformation Roman Catholic Chapel in Newcastle. The street houses St Andrew's Roman Catholic Church, the porch window of which contains some glass from his first chapel, which was built in Pilgrim Street in 1798.

Top) Sixties' fashions seen on High Bridge. Right)
The old Northern bus station on Worswick Street

Mosley Street

One of the first results of the Newcastle Streets Act 1784 was the building of a new street to facilitate East-West communication. The Minute Book of Newcastle Common Council records that a meeting held on 14th April 1785, "Ordered that the new street leading out of the Flesh Market into Pilgrim Street be called Mosley Street out of respect for the exertions of Mr Alderman Mosley in promoting material improvement of the Town". In 1818 it was the first street in Newcastle to be lit using gas lamps. The original Theatre Royal fronted onto Mosley Street before the building of Grey Street.

Compare the 1900 image on the right to the modern day street scene below.

Grey Street

Built over the Lort Burn as the central part of Grainger-Dobson improvements, this street was originally called Upper Dean Street. It was named Grey Street in the 1830s after the second Earl Grey, whose seat was at Howick Hall in Northumberland. He was Prime Minister and a very popular personality in the North East. Its focal point, the Grey Monument, designed by Benjamin Green, remains one of the most prominent landmarks in the city. It commemorates Grey's Reform Act of 1832, which extended voting rights (but by no means to everyone) and ended some of the corruption of the old system. The monument is 135 feet high and was completed in August 1838 with a statue of Earl Grey by Baillie. Earl Grey's head is somewhat newer. The original was struck off by lightning in 1941 and a replacement was made in 1947. The Theatre Royal was built in Grey Street by John and Benjamin Green in 1837.

Above: 1) Grey Street in 1860. 2) The Grey Street Picture House in 1930. 3) Grey Street decorated in 1953.
Next page) Grey Street in 1900.

Drury Lane

Newcastle's first Theatre Royal was built in 1788 on Mosley Street and stood slightly to the east of the present Drury Lane. The street was called after its London counterpart where another Theatre Royal stands. The theatre was demolished in the 1830s when Richard Grainger developed Grey Street and promised to put up a new theatre there.

Collingwood Street

Collingwood Street was opened in 1810 to extend the through route from Pilgrim Street to Westgate. It was named after Lord Cuthbert Collingwood, who was born at the head of Side in 1748. He died in 1810, five years after his heroic action at the Battle of Trafalgar where he took command after the death of Admiral Lord Nelson. Collingwood was educated at the Newcastle Royal Grammar School under its distinguished headmaster, Hugh Moises. There are two monuments to him; one in Saint Nicholas's Cathedral, the other at Tynemouth, overlooking the mouth of the river.

The Bigg Market, Cloth Market, Groat Market

Newcastle had many markets, which were held by Royal Licence in the Quayside area and in the area around St Nicholas's church. Bigg Market extended from Newgate Street towards the church, splitting at its south, until the mid-19th century, into three streets: from east to west Cloth Market, Middle Street and Groat Market. Bigg is a particular kind of barley that has four rows of grain on each ear, which was presumably sold on the Bigg Market. The market was also used for hirings for farm servants, and carriers' carts would come in from the countryside. In 1858 Middle Street was demolished for a new Town Hall to be built between Cloth Market and Groat Market.

Before the Grainger Market was built, the area now known as the Cloth Market consisted of the Flesh Market, the Fish Market and the Cloth Market. Every August and October, dealers in blankets and linen set up stalls or booths here. One of the best known establishments in the Cloth Market is Balmbra's Music Hall, which is immortalised in the Geordie Anthem, *The Blaydon Races*.

The Groat Market was so called because this was the place where grains and wheat were sold. It was established here by 1743. A groat in Northumberland dialect means wheat. Groats are oats with husks removed but not ground. The street also contained numerous shops and inns. The Town Post House was here too, at its junction with Pudding Chare. Thomas Bewick often drank in the Black Boy Inn, which is still standing.

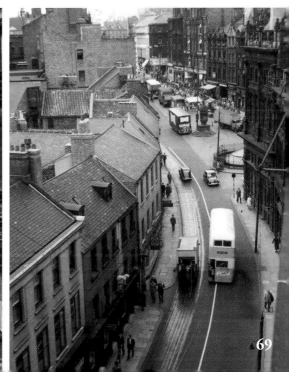

Pudding Chare

Newcastle historian Henry Bourne claimed that this street was originally called Budding Chare. However, the Reverend Collingwood Bruce, in his handbook of 1863, suggests that the street was also called because vendors of Black Puddings had their stalls here. The name could be derived from a nearby hidden stream High or Pow Dene. Heslop's Glossary mentions the intestine-like winding and narrow nature of the lane and associates this with pudding. Nobody can really know the true origins of such an old name.

This image from 1929 shows the medieval layout though very little of that survives today. Part of the Mining Institute and Neville Hall can be seen on Westgate Road at the end of Pudding Chare.

From City Road to East Quayside

Dean Street

Before 1784, the main route from the Tyne Bridge to the busy market areas of Newcastle or to the north was by way of Side, or up the precipitous valley of the Lort Burn. Pack horses could cope, but carts and carriages could not. Between the years 1784 and 1789 the lower part of the valley was filled in and Dean Street was built by David Stephenson. It takes its name from the dene that lies beneath it.

2444 DEAN STREET, NEWCASTLE.

Low Bridge

Before the valley of the Lort Burn was filled, two bridges crossed this lower part, the site of which is now occupied by Grey Street and Dean Street. While High Bridge linked Bigg Market with Pilgrim Street, the Nether Dean Bridge or Low Bridge linked Pilgrim Street to Saint Nicholas's churchyard and its site is commemorated by the stairs marked Low Bridge leading up to the Tyne Bridge. Low Bridge was removed in 1787.

Lombard Street

After the great fire in 1854, which destroyed much of the Quayside, the area was rebuilt. Lombard Street was built in 1863 and was probably named after its London counterpart because this was the business centre of Newcastle. The image shows Lombard Street in around 1970, the Tyne Bridge is on the right.

Queen Street and King Street

With Lombard Street, these streets were designed by John Dobson to form an elegant area to replace the 'chares' lost in the fire of 1854. There had been streets with these names adjacent to the Keep but they were removed in the building of the High Level Bridge. The steps up Akenside Hill and Dog Bank give a dramatic view of All Saints' Church.

Akenside Hill and Dog Bank

Akenside Hill was originally called All Hallows Lane, then known as Butcher Bank (it was traditionally inhabited by butchers who worked in the nearby Flesh Market). A more genteel name was suggested by Alderman William Lockley Harle, a 19th century reformer. The street name commemorates the life of Mark Akenside who was born there in 1721. Although lamed in early life, Akenside was able to pursue a successful medical career as well as being a well-known poet of the day. He died in 1770. Dog Bank, which means a narrow twisted lane (a dog leg) continued east from the foot of Pilgrim Street.

Silver Street

This lane, situated just north of All Saints' Church, takes its name from the silver merchants who lived in the area. The street had previously been known as Jew Gate, Temple Gate and All Hallowgate (All Saints' earlier name was All Hallows). The Reverend Henry Bourne (born in 1694 in Newcastle), the famous historian, was Curate at All Saints' Church from 1722 until his death in 1733.

Above and left: Silver Street - in the older picture you can faintly see the Sallyport Tower, the view is obscured by trees in 2017.
Top and right: On Akenside Hill, the steep bank leading up to All Saints' Church.

Manor Chare and Manors

After the dissolution of the monasteries in 1539, Henry VIII kept the Augustinian Priory, which was on the site of the Holy Jesus Hospital, as the office of the Council in the North. It became known as the King's Manor, the corruption of which name has survived. Manor Chare led to Holy Jesus Hospital from Broad Chare via Austin Chare (Austin is a corruption of Augustinian). The Corporation of Newcastle built the Holy Jesus Hospital in 1681 to house the poor and infirm Freeman and their widows. In 1884 each inmate was provided with coal, clothing and five shillings per week.

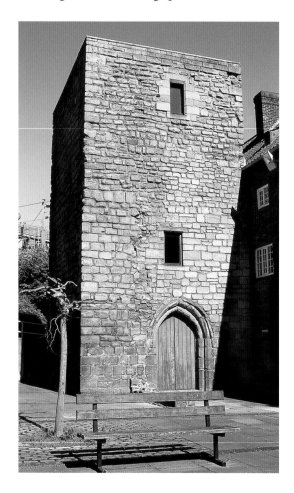

City Road

In 1400, when Henry IV granted a charter to the town, Newcastle became a county in its own right. It was not until 1882, however, that Newcastle became a city. At the same time the Diocese of Newcastle was carved out of the Diocese of Durham. The former Parish church of Saint Nicholas became the new cathedral. At this time the lower part of Pandon Dene was being filled in to improve the New Road built in 1776 from Milk Market to North Shields. To honour Newcastle's new status, this road was renamed City Road when it was opened in 1882.

Pandon Bank

Pandon was originally a separate township from Newcastle but in 1299 Newcastle annexed Pandon, making it part of the town. The Town Wall was built eastwards from the Corner Tower to take in this new property. Pandon Gate, which stood in the section of the Town Wall between Corner Tower and Wall Knoll (or Sallyport) Tower, was demolished in 1795.

This image of 1897 shows the Home for Destitute Boys.

Sandgate and Milk Market

In Sandgate lived most of the keelmen, who rowed their flat-bottomed boats or keels loaded with coal from the staiths on the river to the waiting collier ships at the mouth of the Tyne. Standing above Sandgate on the City Road is the only remaining memorial to the keelmen – the Keelmen's Hospital. The keelmen raised the money to build the hospital, opened in 1701, to care for aged keelmen and their families. The Sandgate was both a street (the sandy road) and a gate in the Town Wall.

As the name suggests, the Milk Market is where the locals in the 19th century bought their milk and meat at a daily market. A famous Newcastle landmark known as the Sandgate Pant (a water fountain) stood just off the Milk Market at the junction with Sandgate.

The Chares of Newcastle Quayside

Until the catastrophic fire in 1854, Newcastle Quayside was crowded with twenty 'chares', narrow streets that led back from the river beginning with Dark Chare in the west and ending with Love Lane in the east. These alleys were packed with dwellings. In 1811, for example, the three houses in Plummer Chare had fifty-three people living in them. The Town Wall ran along the riverside until after the mid-18th century. The word chare is derived from the Anglo-Saxon 'cer' or 'cerre' meaning a turning. The chares often had names reflecting their appearance or owners. Those lost in the fire included Grinden Chare, Blue Anchor Chare, Peppercorn Chare, Pallister's Chare, Colvin's Chare and Hornsby's Chare. The west Quayside was rebuilt by John Dobson but eleven chares remain including the following:

Byker Chare

In the Middle Ages Robert de Byker and his wife Laderine owned large estates around Newcastle including parts of Pandon. This chare, and the suburb of Byker, is probably named after him.

Cocks Chare

The name of this chare simply derives from Alderman Cocks who lived here.

Custom House Yard

In 1766 the Customs House was moved from the west end of the Quayside to the present site. The present building dates from the 1840s and Sidney Smirk, son-in-law of the more famous John Dobson, designed the facade. The Customs House reflects Newcastle's former commercial importance and has given its name to this chare.

Fenwick's Entry

Alderman Cuthbert Fenwick lived here and the street was named after him. The image on the right shows Fenwick's Entry in 1967.

Plummer Chare

Plummer Chare is named after Robert Plummer, one of the bailiffs of Newcastle in 1378, whose house was on this site. Plummer Tower is preserved on Croft Street. The image on the right shows Plummer Chare in the 70s, the building on the left of the chare is now Sabatini's restuarant.

Trinity Chare

Trinity House, off Broad Chare, and also approached by Trinity Chare, became the home of the Fellowship of the Masters and Mariners of the ships of the town of Newcastle upon Tyne, the Guild and Fraternity of the Blessed Trinity, in 1505 when they were granted permission to build a chapel, meeting house and almhouses there. Trinity House became responsible for lighthouses in 1536, and for pilotage in the region. In return they were permitted to levy tolls and fees on ships trading in the Tyne.

Broad Chare

Broad Chare, although narrow by modern standards, was named because it was the only chare down which a cart could pass. It was widened again when the buildings between it and Spicer Chare were removed. The Quayside Law Courts stand on the site of Spicer Chare.